NATIONAL
GEOGRAPHIC

W9-CAU-485

From Hive to Home

Isabella Jose

Contents

Do you like **honey**?

Do you know where honey comes from?

Honeybees

Honey comes from **honeybees**.
Honeybees make honey from **nectar**.
Nectar is a sweet liquid that flowers make.

Honeybees collect the nectar from flowers.
They take the nectar back to the **hive**.

Honeybees keep the nectar in a **honeycomb**. The bees seal the honeycomb with **wax** they make from their bodies.

The nectar gets thick inside the honeycomb.
The nectar turns into honey.

Beekeepers are people who keep bees. They often sell the honey their bees make.

Beekeepers keep bees in a special wooden box.
The bees live in the box the same way they live in a hive.
The bees make honey inside the box.

When the honeycomb is full of honey, the beekeeper takes it out of the box.

The beekeeper must wear a special hat and long gloves.

These clothes protect the beekeeper from bee stings.

Honey for Sale

The beekeeper cuts the wax off the honeycomb.

The honeycomb is put into a machine.
The machine spins the honeycomb.
Spinning pulls the honey out of the honeycomb.

The honey is cleaned and put into large tanks. Then, the honey is poured into jars.

People can buy the jars of honey.

Glossary

beekeeper	a person who keep bees
hive	place where bees live
honey	a thick, sweet liquid made by bees from flower nectar
honeybee	a bee that makes honey from nectar
honeycomb	the part of the hive that holds honey
nectar	a sweet liquid that flowers make
wax	material bees use to seal the honeycomb